NO LONGER KEEPING THE PEACE

AN INVITATION FOR RECONCILIATION AFTER
SEXUAL VIOLENCE WITHIN THE CHURCH

SAM HOUSER

TEHOM
CENTER

Copyright © 2024 by Sam Houser

All rights reserved.

No part of this book may be reproduced in any form or by any electronic or mechanical means, including information storage and retrieval systems, without written permission from the author, except for the use of brief quotations in a book review.

Tehom Center Publishing is a 501(c)3 nonprofit publishing feminist and queer authors, with a commitment to elevate BIPOC writers. Its face and voice is Rev. Dr. Angela Yarber.

Paperback ISBN: 979-8-9914844-6-6

Ebook ISBN: 979-8-9914844-7-3

To all those who have been silenced, who have not had the opportunity, privilege, or safety to use their voices, I dedicate this work to you.

For those who have been forced to 'keep the peace' at the expense of their own truth, I see you. The phrase 'keeping the peace' is often wielded as a tool by those who would rather ignore the problem than confront the conflict. But peace without justice is no peace at all.

This book is for you, in the hope that one day your voice will break through the silence.

CONTENTS

Acknowledgments	vii
Author's Note	ix
1. Preparing to Listen	1
2. Understanding the Need for a Healing Cycle to Get Through This Book	5
3. Upholding Equity, Addressing Pay Inequality	15
4. Liberating Voices, Honoring Identity	27
5. Cultivating Sacred Allyship	41
6. Systemic Harassment	51
7. Perpetuated Harm through Assault	65
Afterword: A Vision of Hope and Change	75

ACKNOWLEDGMENTS

To my amazingly supportive spouse, Dustin and my four tenacious children who have felt the deep impact of the violence I've endured at the hands of the church, this work is an acknowledgment of the reconciling journey we have all been on together. Your love and resilience has been my foundation.

To my dearest friend and unwavering supporter, The Reverend Becky Pagone, you held up a mirror of courage that was impossible to look away from and handed me a microphone of fearlessness that I dared not drop. Your faith in me, your insistence that I could face the darkness, has been the light guiding this journey. Without you, along with the tender support of First Congregational UCC in Sioux Falls, this story would still be hidden.

Thank you for bearing witness to the hardest of moments, for holding onto faith when mine faltered.

AUTHOR'S NOTE

In the pages that follow, you will embark on a transformative journey through the intersections of trauma, faith, and healing. This book was written for those who have found themselves entangled in the tension between sacred spaces and human failings—for the leaders who stand at the pulpit, for the women who have carried the weight of injustice, and for the believers who have felt both called and silenced. It's for those who have been wounded by the very institution meant to offer refuge, and for the bystanders who never saw the harm until it was too late. Whether you are someone longing for healing, someone reckoning with your role in the cycle of harm, or a faithful soul committed to justice, this book is an invitation. It calls on each of us to engage in deep reflection and courageous conversations about the brokenness that lingers in sacred places. It is written with the hope that we might together step into a more expansive, grace-filled future—one where reconciliation is not a distant dream but an embodied reality for all who seek it.

It is with great humility and deep awareness of my own identity that I invite you to explore this narrative. I am a white, neuro-divergent, non-binary, socially informed female, raised in a middle-class environment and currently residing in that socio-economic status.

My life is shaped by the loving presence of my four children and supportive spouse. It is within this context that I bring forth this piece of work—a compass to navigate the depths of trauma within the Christian tradition and to illuminate the path toward healing.

As I embarked on this writing endeavor, I recognized that the complexity of human experience could not be confined to a single perspective. Trauma, after all, does not discriminate. It permeates the lives of individuals across diverse backgrounds, cultures, and belief systems. It is a pervasive force that respects no boundaries. Therefore, it is crucial to acknowledge the limitations of my own experience and positionality, while simultaneously honoring the countless narratives that intersect with and diverge from my own.

The words that fill these pages emerge from a place of lived experience, compassion, and an unwavering commitment to social justice. I have witnessed the profound impact of trauma within the Christian tradition—a sacred space where individuals seek solace, guidance, and connection. Yet, it is within this very tradition that trauma can often go unacknowledged or be shrouded in silence. Through extensive research, reflective introspection, and conversations with individuals who have embarked on their own healing journeys, I have woven together a tapestry of insights, stories, and practices that invite you to confront the shadows of trauma and embrace the transformative power of healing.

This guide is not a prescriptive roadmap, but rather a gentle companion. It invites you to explore the depths of your own pain, to engage with the intricate webs of trauma that have touched your life, and to uncover the pathways that lead toward liberation and wholeness. It seeks to hold space for the diverse and nuanced experiences within the Christian tradition, acknowledging the ways in which trauma has impacted individuals at various levels—physically, emotionally, and spiritually. It is my hope that these words will serve as a catalyst for conversations, fostering empathy, understanding, and ultimately, collective healing.

As we journey together through these pages, I invite you to approach this guide with an open heart, a willingness to wrestle with difficult truths, and a deep longing for healing. May it empower you to embrace your own story, honor your pain, and cultivate resilience. May it offer solace to those who have carried the weight of trauma within the Christian tradition, assuring them that they are not alone. And may it inspire a collective awakening—a transformation that extends far beyond the confines of these words, and into a world that is ripe for healing and redemption.

With love and compassion,
Sam

1

PREPARING TO LISTEN

> The courageous conversation is the one you don't want to have
>
> DAVID WHYTE

Dear readers of all genders, but specifically my testosterone fed bodied readers…

As you embark on the journey through this book, you will encounter narratives that might be difficult to read—stories of pain, injustice, and the persistent challenges faced by women, particularly those in ministry. These are not just stories; they are lived experiences, each one a reflection of the harsh realities that many women in the church endure. This chapter is specifically for you, the male reader, to help you engage with these narratives in a way that is not only respectful but also constructive. It is about preparing your heart and mind to be an ally in a world where the voices of women, especially those in spiritual leadership, are often marginalized, dismissed, unheard, and worse, violently silenced.

To start, it is crucial to acknowledge that the stories shared in this book are not isolated incidents or exaggerated accounts. They are the lived realities of countless women who have been subjected to harassment, discrimination, and violence simply because of their gender and gender expression. As a man, or one that presents masculine, you may not have personally experienced these kinds of injustices, and that can make it difficult to fully grasp their severity. However, your role as a reader is to approach these stories with an open heart and a willingness to believe what is being shared.

Many male readers, especially those who might not have firsthand experience with the injustices women face, may find themselves questioning the stories and information they are about to engage with. It's not uncommon for a sense of disbelief to arise—thoughts like "This can't be the norm" or "Surely this is exaggerated" might come to mind. As you navigate these narratives, you may feel defensive, perhaps even offended, particularly if the experiences shared contrast sharply with your own understanding of the church or your experiences as a man. However, this book is not written to provoke anger or defensiveness. Instead, it's an invitation—a call to broaden your perspective, to step into the shoes of others, particularly women in ministry, and to listen with an open heart and mind. The discomfort you may feel is not meant to alienate you but to prompt deeper reflection and a more empathetic response.

This is not about questioning the validity of these experiences or comparing them to your own. It's about recognizing that the pain expressed in these chapters is real and that it demands your attention and empathy. When you read about pay inequality, microaggressions, harassment, or assault, understand that these are systemic issues that affect women across all fields, including the church. They are not the result of a few bad actors; they are embedded in the very fabric of many institutions, often perpetuated unconsciously by those who benefit from the status quo. That includes the church.

Digging Deeper

One of the most important things you can do as a male reader is to resist the urge to become defensive. You will be triggered throughout this book and I ask that when your critical thinking starts to diminish you make space to remember that this book is not about you and therefore YOU can keep showing up.

Remember that it's natural to feel uncomfortable when confronted with accounts of gender-based injustice, especially if you've never consciously participated in it. You might feel the need to defend yourself or your male colleagues, to insist that "not all men" are guilty of these behaviors. While this reaction is understandable, it is not helpful.

Instead, try to sit with the discomfort. Allow yourself to feel it, and then let it move you to a place of empathy rather than defensiveness. Understand that these stories are not indictments of all men, but rather invitations to all men to become part of the solution. By listening without defensiveness, you open yourself up to the possibility of learning and growing as an ally.

And as you read, take time to reflect on your own attitudes and behaviors. Ask yourself: Have I ever unknowingly, or unknowingly participated in or perpetuated a culture that diminishes the voices and experiences of women? Have I ever dismissed a woman's perspective or failed to take her concerns seriously? Have I been a passive bystander in situations where I should have spoken up?

These are hard questions, but they are necessary if you are to engage in meaningful allyship. Recognize that becoming an ally is not a one-time act but a lifelong commitment to challenging both your own biases and the structures that uphold inequality. It requires humility, a willingness to learn from your mistakes, and the courage to make changes in your own life and within your community.

Next Steps

After reading the stories in this book, you may feel compelled to discuss them with others—whether that's in your church, your workplace, or your social circles. These conversations are essential, but they must be approached with care. It's important to enter these discussions with a mindset of listening rather than leading. Remember, your role as a male ally is not to dominate the conversation but to support and amplify the voices of women.

When you do speak, focus on asking questions rather than offering solutions. Encourage those around you to share their experiences and insights, and be mindful of the power dynamics that can often silence women's voices in mixed-gender settings. By creating space for these voices to be heard, you contribute to a culture of respect and equality.

Finally, it's vital to understand that the issues discussed in this book are not limited to the church or any single field. Gender-based injustice is a widespread problem that affects women in every profession, every community, and every corner of the world. The stories you read here are a window into a much larger issue, one that requires the collective efforts of all genders to address.

By educating yourself, engaging in self-reflection, and participating in conversations about these issues, you take an important step toward being part of the change. This book is not just about exposing the problems; it's about inspiring solutions and fostering a community where all people—regardless of gender—are treated with dignity and respect.

If you've made it this far, congratulations…as you move forward, carry these lessons with you. Approach the stories with humility, engage with empathy, and commit to being an active ally in the fight against gender-based injustice. The journey may be challenging, but it is one that will ultimately lead to a more just and equitable world for everyone.

2

UNDERSTANDING THE NEED FOR A HEALING CYCLE TO GET THROUGH THIS BOOK

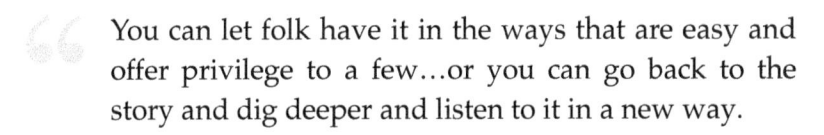

> You can let folk have it in the ways that are easy and offer privilege to a few…or you can go back to the story and dig deeper and listen to it in a new way.
>
> PHYLLIS TRIBLE

Matthew 18: 15-20, The Message

"If a fellow believer hurts you, go and tell him—work it out between the two of you. If he listens, you've made a friend. If he won't listen, take one or two others along so that the presence of witnesses will keep things honest, and try again. If he still won't listen, tell the church. If he won't listen to the church, you'll have to start over from scratch, confront him with the need for repentance, and offer again God's forgiving love.

"Take this most seriously: A yes on earth is yes in heaven; a no on earth is no in heaven. What you say to one another is eternal. I mean this. When two of you get together on anything at all on earth and make a prayer of it, my Father in heaven goes into action. And when two or three of you are together because of me, you can be sure that I'll be there."

Digging Deeper

The piece of scripture that this chapter begins with is often quoted in discussions about resolving disputes. It can, and has been read as a procedural roadmap for handling disagreements and breaches within the church. The verses from the Gospel of Matthew outline a process: addressing the issue directly with the individual, bringing witnesses if necessary, involving the church if needed, and ultimately seeking repentance and reconciliation. However, the essence of this scripture goes beyond a mere procedural guide. It is fundamentally about accountability—an invitation to embody the principles of honesty, justice, and communal responsibility.

The primary focus of Matthew 18:15-20 is not on following a strict set of steps but on fostering a culture of accountability and integrity within the faith community. The passage underscores the importance of addressing wrongs and conflicts with a spirit of love and commitment to justice. It encourages believers to engage in honest and transparent dialogue, ensuring that conflicts are resolved with fairness and respect.

The passage's emphasis on accountability is evident in the call for repentance and reconciliation. Jesus does not prescribe a rigid formula for resolution but rather highlights the importance of addressing issues openly and seeking genuine reconciliation. The involvement of witnesses and the church is meant to ensure that the process remains honest and just, rather than turning into a bureaucratic or punitive system. This approach is about creating a community where every member holds each other accountable and strives for mutual respect and understanding.

Matthew 18:15-20 is a reminder that the health of a community depends on its ability to address conflicts with integrity and compassion. It calls believers to a higher standard of accountability, where actions and words are held to the principles of truth and love. The passage encourages believers to work together to resolve issues and seek forgiveness, fostering a community where every member is valued and respected.

In practical terms, this means that when conflicts arise, the focus should be on genuine reconciliation rather than adhering to a step-by-step procedure. The scripture invites us to engage deeply with one another, to listen and understand, and to act in ways that reflect our commitment to justice and love. It is less about following a set process and more about cultivating a community where accountability and reconciliation are core values.

When applied to situations of abuse or systemic injustice, this passage challenges us to approach such issues with a commitment to accountability and justice. It calls for addressing abuse with the seriousness it deserves and ensuring that all actions are guided by principles of fairness and empathy. The goal is not to follow a mechanical process but to foster an environment where every individual is treated with dignity and respect.

In addressing abuse within the church, Matthew 18:15-20 encourages us to hold perpetrators accountable while providing support and healing for victims. It underscores the need for a community that does not shy away from confronting wrongs but does so in a manner that upholds the values of justice, compassion, and integrity.

Matthew 18:15-20, often interpreted as a step-by-step guide to addressing harm, can feel impossible to follow for someone who has been abused, especially when the power dynamics are stacked against them. For a victim of abuse, the idea of confronting their perpetrator directly can evoke overwhelming fear and paralysis. When those in power are involved, the stakes become even higher, and the expectation to engage with their abuser in a vulnerable dialogue feels not only unsafe but deeply unjust. But this scripture, when read through a lens of compassion, is not about demanding face-to-face confrontation in every circumstance. Rather, it invites us to create systems of accountability where the burden is not placed solely on the victim to seek resolution. It calls for faith communities to cultivate environments of transparency, safety, and collective responsibility. True accountability means recognizing the complexities of power and abuse, and ensuring that harm is addressed with care, justice, and a deep respect for the well-being of the wounded. This way, we honor the heart of the passage—not through rigid procedure, but through our shared commitment to healing and restoration.

Finding Meaning

In a world where the church is often seen as a sanctuary of hope and redemption, it is disheartening to acknowledge the deep-seated patriarchal structures that have marginalized women for centuries. The very institution that preaches equality, love, and justice has, at times, upheld systems of abuse and discrimination, creating a crisis of faith and trust. This chapter embarks on a profound journey of reconciliation, drawing inspiration from Andy Johns' healing progression model, which you will find outlined in the next few pages. By navigating through the stages of crisis, equilibrium, understanding, awareness, confrontation, transcendence, incineration, liminality, rebuilding, and arrival, we seek to illuminate a path toward true healing and transformation.

This journey is not merely about addressing past wrongs but about forging a new identity rooted in genuine equality and respect. It is a call to the church to rise from the ashes of its patriarchal past and embrace a future where every member, regardless of gender, is valued and empowered. The road to reconciliation is arduous, but it is a necessary pilgrimage for a community that professes faith in a redeemer. By committing to this process, the church can embody the redemption it proclaims and become a beacon of hope and justice in the world.

Next Steps

Looking at the process of reconciliation through the lens of a healing journey there are procedures that are designed to keep us in relationship. Below are the stages of healing that this book will offer interwoven within each chapter so that those who are engaged in the work of reconciliation can remain in relationship while healing individually with the goal of healing institutionally.

Crisis: When the Bottom Drops Out

This is where it all falls apart. Think of it as the moment the rug is pulled out from under you, and you're left gasping on the cold, hard floor. Sometimes, it's an abrupt, soul-crushing event that yanks the blinders off. Other times, it's the slow erosion of trust and belonging, eroded over years until the ground crumbles. The church, often seen as a sanctuary, reveals its underbelly of sexism, and women in ministry face the blunt force of systemic patriarchy. Here, fear, rage, and hopelessness take center stage, and rational thinking goes on a hiatus. The church community can either crash and burn or seize this rock-bottom moment as a launching pad for something better, something real.

Equilibrium: Finding Your Sea Legs

When you're in the throes of a crisis, all you crave is solid ground. In this phase, the church is desperate for something steady to cling to. We're talking about survival mode, grabbing at anything that offers a glimmer of safety and normalcy. This might mean creating immediate, tangible changes like new policies, safe spaces, and open dialogue. It's about piecing together a semblance of stability. The goal here is not just to patch things up but to find a new normal that doesn't suck. It's pulling away from harmful dynamics and might mean stepping away from toxic influences or seeking external help. Equilibrium is about re-establishing a foundation that actually supports everyone, not just the status quo.

Understanding: Peeling Back the Layers

With some semblance of stability, the church can finally start to breathe and think. Now, it's time to dig deep and understand how we got here. This isn't about blame games but about real, raw insight. Why has patriarchy thrived in these sacred spaces? The community dives into the history, theology, and social constructs that have woven sexism into the church's fabric. This stage is about education and awareness, facilitated through workshops, discussions, and teachings that challenge old narratives. The church starts to see the bigger picture, recognizing the intricate web of influences that led to the crisis. Understanding lays the groundwork for genuine healing and transformation.

Awareness: Seeing with New Eyes

Once we get a handle on the intellectual side of things, it's time to go deeper. Awareness is about self-reflection and honesty. The church must look in the mirror and ask the hard questions: How have we been complicit? What subconscious biases are at play? This phase involves a lot of uncomfortable but necessary introspection. Through guided meditations, reflective journaling, and heart-to-heart conversations, members start to recognize their own roles in perpetuating inequality. This heightened awareness allows the church to catch and correct destructive patterns. It's a collective awakening, a movement from ignorance to enlightenment, fostering a community that's more empathetic and aligned with its core values.

Confrontation: Facing the Ugly Truths

With awareness comes the responsibility to act. The church

must now confront the ugly truths head-on. This is where we call out the specific incidents, beliefs, and structures that have hurt women. It's messy and painful, but it's also liberating. This stage demands transparency and accountability. Apologies are made, wrongs are righted, and policies are reformed. The community commits to tackling these issues openly, no more sweeping things under the rug. Confrontation is about facing the demons of patriarchy, knowing that only through this struggle can true healing begin. It's the moment we decide to stop running from the truth and start building something better.

Transcendence: Rising Above the Fray

Having faced the storm, the church now begins to transcend its past limitations. This isn't just about change; it's about transformation. The community embraces a new identity, free from the shackles of patriarchy. It's a period of growth and renewal, where the church starts to live out its values in a more authentic way. Doctrines are revised, leadership structures become more inclusive, and the culture shifts towards one of genuine equality. This stage is about moving forward with a clear vision and purpose, shedding old skins and stepping into a brighter, more inclusive future. It's a journey of liberation, where the church becomes a beacon of hope and justice.

Incineration: Burning Down the Old

To fully embrace this new identity, the church must go through a process of incineration. This is where we burn down the remnants of the old, patriarchal ways. It sounds radical, but it's necessary. This means letting go of practices, traditions, and mindsets that no longer serve our commitment to gender equality. It's a cleansing fire, making way for new growth. This stage is about making room for the new by consciously and decisively abandoning the old. It's a symbolic and practical step, ensuring that the church's future is not weighed down by the past. By letting go of what no longer serves, the church prepares for rebirth.

Liminality: The Grey Zone

After incineration, the church finds itself in a liminal space – the grey zone. This is a period of ambiguity and transition, where the old ways are gone, but the new haven't fully taken shape. It's an in-between phase that can feel uncertain and unsettling. But it's also a time of potential and exploration. The church must be open to new possibilities and willing to experiment with different practices, structures, and relationships. This is a time for reflection and creativity, where the community reimagines its future and lays the groundwork for lasting change. Liminality is a space of becoming, where the church navigates the unknown with hope and courage.

Rebuilding: Crafting a New Path

With lessons learned and insights gained, the church embarks on the process of rebuilding. This stage is about creating a new, inclusive, and equitable community. The church actively works to establish policies, programs, and practices that support the full participation and leadership of women. This might include mentorship programs, gender-neutral language in worship, and transparent decision-making processes. The rebuilding phase is marked by intentionality and collaboration, drawing on the strengths and contributions of all members. By crafting its own path, the church not only heals from the wounds of patriarchy but also becomes a beacon of hope and justice for others. This is a time of bold, fearless creation, where the church steps into its true potential.

Arrival: A New Dawn

Finally, the church reaches a point of arrival, where the journey of healing and transformation culminates in a new, vibrant reality.

The community looks back on its past struggles with a sense of gratitude for the growth and wisdom gained. The demons of patriarchy have been confronted and overcome, leaving the church stronger and more resilient. This arrival is not an end but a new beginning, where the church lives out its commitment to gender equality in every aspect of its existence. The path forward is guided by a vision of justice, inclusion, and love, as the church continues to evolve and thrive. With each step, the church moves closer to its ideal, embodying the sacred allyship that uplifts and empowers all its members.

As readers who are committed to the bold work of reconciliation regarding the abuse and harm done to and against women in the church, you stand at the threshold of a transformative journey. The healing progression model laid out by Andy Johns offers a roadmap for the church to navigate its reconciliation with the wounds of patriarchy. Each stage, from the heart-wrenching crisis to the hopeful arrival, is a step towards dismantling oppressive systems and building a community grounded in love, equality, and justice.

The undeniable need for reconciliation within the church is not just a moral imperative but a reflection of its core beliefs. To proclaim a redeemer while perpetuating systems of oppression is a contradiction that must be resolved. The church's credibility, its witness to the world, and its ability to be a true sanctuary depend on its willingness to confront and heal from its patriarchal legacy.

By embracing this journey, the church can transform from a place of pain and exclusion to one of healing and inclusion. It is a journey that requires courage, honesty, and a steadfast commitment to justice. Let us move forward with the conviction that reconciliation is not just possible but essential. In doing so, we honor the spirit of redemption that lies at the heart of our faith and create a church that truly reflects the inclusive love of the redeemer we profess to follow.

References

Johns, A. (2023, July 24). *The stages of emotional healing.* Clues to Life. https://cluesdotlife.substack.com/p/the-stages-of-emotional-healing

Resources

The Sound Healing Academy (https://www.academyofsoundhealing.com/)
Association of Nature and Forest Therapy Guides and Programs (https://www.natureandforesttherapy.org/)
Somatic Experiencing® Trauma Institute (https://traumahealing.org/)
National Center for Trauma-Informed Care (NCTIC) (https://www.samhsa.gov/trauma-violence-types)

3

UPHOLDING EQUITY, ADDRESSING PAY INEQUALITY

> It is no measure of health to be well adjusted to a profoundly sick society.
>
> JIDDU KRISHNAMURTI

Mak's story

Mak was a mid-career, white woman receiving a call to a new judicatory position along with two other, male presenting colleagues in ministry. Mak had gone through the interview process, understood the role, negotiated for a salary that felt fair given the outline of responsibilities and began work. A few months into the new job Mak learned that she was making $5,000 less than her male counterpart even though Mak had the additional task of supervision of other staff. Mak addressed this with the board chair and was told that those decisions weren't the board's to make or discuss.

Mak was left wondering how advocating for pay equality with

the sole head of staff might impact her job stability, the dynamics between her and the head of staff, and the dynamics between her and the other staff.

Digging Deeper

One of the most pervasive issues of misogyny in the work force is that of pay inequality. Mak's story highlights that there is nuance to the inequities that show up in ministry that may very well correlate to the secular world, but our focus is to look at the intricate web of financial disparities and the profound repercussions on women's emotional, spiritual, and overall well-being through a lens informed by religious values of human dignity and inherent worth...since we are talking about the harm that happens within a religious system. As we work through this multifaceted topic the aim is to advocate for transformative change rooted in justice and compassion by shedding light on the immediate and long-term consequences of pay inequality.

What we know is that women, on average, continue to earn significantly less than their male counterparts, with women of color experiencing even wider disparities. According to a report by the Institute for Women's Policy Research (IWPR), in 2021, women earned only 82 cents for every dollar earned by men, and the gap is even more pronounced for women of color, with Black women earning 63 cents and Hispanic women earning 57 cents for every dollar earned by white men. This financial divide denies women equitable compensation for their labor and expertise, perpetuating an unjust system that erodes their sense of worth and equality. Such disparities can cause long term self-doubt as well as reinforce the unworthiness that many women wrestle with wholistically, there is more on these topics later in the book.

Often overlooked is the fact that being clergy is still being an employee, subject to the same economic realities and expectations as any other worker. Clergy members, regardless of their religious vocation, must meet basic family needs and adhere to employment expectations, such as providing for their families, saving for retirement, and managing healthcare costs. The financial stress caused by pay inequality can profoundly impact their personal lives and their ability to serve their congregations effectively. Just like any employee, clergy require fair compensation to maintain their well-being and fulfill their professional and familial responsibilities.

Salary discrepancies for clergy, based on implicit bias around gender, has remained a prevalent concern even amid progressive steps taken to address the reality. In 2016, the Religion News Service revealed data from the Bureau of Labor Statistics showing that female clergy members earned only 76 cents for every dollar earned by their male counterparts—a disheartening reality that reflects a national trend of gender-based wage disparities. This stark figure is especially troubling within the context of religious institutions that often champion values of equality, justice, and compassion.

One might expect progressive congregations, which advocate for gender equality and social justice, to perform better in this area. Unfortunately, they too fall far short. Despite their professed commitments to inclusivity, many progressive congregations still exhibit significant pay gaps between male and female clergy. This suggests that implicit biases and systemic structures continue to undermine efforts toward genuine equality. The persistence of these disparities in even the most forward-thinking religious communities underscores the depth of the problem and the need for continued, intentional action.

The expectation that progressive congregations would lead the way in eliminating pay inequality is not unwarranted. These communities often engage in social justice initiatives and advocate for marginalized groups. However, the data reveals a sobering reality: despite their outward commitments, many have not yet fully addressed the internal, systemic issues that perpetuate gender-based wage disparities. This failure not only impacts the financial stability of female clergy but also signals a broader inconsistency in living out the values of justice and equality that these congregations espouse. Addressing this issue is essential for maintaining integrity and trust within these communities and for ensuring that all clergy are treated with the dignity and respect they deserve.

While some progress has been made, with the gap slightly narrowing in subsequent years, challenges continue. Even when accounting for factors such as education, experience, theological training, and expectations for roles, the wage gap stubbornly persists, underscoring the systemic nature of this inequality. Moreover, unique dynamics within church and ministry contexts further compound the issue. The preference for male leadership, theological beliefs surrounding women's roles, and semantics surrounding job titles can all contribute to discrepancies in pay, leaving many women undervalued and undercompensated for their labor within the church.

It's essential to recognize that the fight for equal pay extends beyond legal battles and administrative actions. The reality is that legal recourse is severely limited due to the ministerial exception, which is why it is so important for individual churches and ministries to understand that they hold significant power in addressing and rectifying pay disparities. Ministerial exception is a legal doctrine that allows religious institutions to make employment decisions about their ministers without interference from the government, even if those decisions would otherwise violate employment laws. It's meant to protect a church's right to choose its leaders according to its faith, but it can also complicate matters when a minister faces issues like harassment or discrimination, as the usual legal protections may not apply. By embracing principles of fairness, transparency in compensation, and equal opportunity, religious institutions can take meaningful steps toward narrowing the gender wage gap and affirming the dignity and worth of all employees, regardless of gender.

While data consistently demonstrates a higher proportion of women than men within the church, the representation of women in clergy positions remains disproportionately low. As of 2016, only 20.7 percent of clergy members were reported to be women, a figure that dwindles further in churches with moderate stances on women's ordination, often restricting them to specific roles. This disparity, coupled with ongoing discrimination against women in religious contexts, contributes to a decline in female church attendance, contrasting with feminist advancements in secular spheres. From 1972 to 2012, regular church attendance among women in the US dropped from 36 percent to 28 percent, while men saw a decline from 26 percent to 22 percent. This trend, expected to worsen among millennials and Generation Z, reflects shifting attitudes toward religious affiliation and gender roles.

The ubiquitous sense of exclusion and marginalization experienced by women in the church stands in stark contrast to the principles of inclusion and equality espoused by Christian teachings. Despite strides made since antiquated views like Saint Thomas Aquinas' assertion of women's inherent inferiority, contemporary church dynamics often perpetuate a hierarchy that subjugates women. Instances of sexism, misogyny, and subtle gender biases undermine the fundamental values of love, justice, and equity upheld by Christianity, reinforcing historical patterns of oppression and discrimination. It is imperative that churches address these systemic issues and cultivate environments where all members, regardless of gender, are valued and respected as equals.

Finding Meaning

Pay inequality exacts a heavy toll on women's emotional well-being. The persistent struggle to make ends meet, combined with the knowledge of being undervalued, creates feelings of frustration, stress, and diminished self-worth. Constantly navigating a system that fails to recognize and reward their contributions can lead to emotional exhaustion and burnout. These emotional consequences not only impact individual women but also reverberate through families and communities.

The spiritual dimension of pay inequality emerges as women question their self-worth and purpose. Feelings of injustice and frustration may challenge their faith, as they wrestle with the dissonance between their spiritual beliefs and lived experiences. The struggle to reconcile their inherent dignity with a system that devalues their contributions can lead to spiritual disconnection and a sense of alienation from religious institutions.

In the sacred texts of various religious traditions, we find teachings that emphasize the importance of justice, compassion, and equality. For example, in the Christian tradition, the Bible speaks of God's call to "do justice, love kindness, and walk humbly" (Micah 6:8), while in Islam, the Quran instructs believers to "stand out firmly for justice, as witnesses to Allah" (Quran 4:135). These teachings remind us of our moral obligation to uphold fairness and equity in all aspects of life, including the realm of finances. Yet, for many clergywomen, the stark discrepancy between these scriptural directives and their lived experiences within the church creates profound stress and internal conflict.

Clergywomen often enter their vocations with a deep sense of calling and commitment to the principles of justice and equality espoused by their faith. They are drawn to ministry by the desire to serve, to lead, and to embody the teachings of their religious traditions. However, when faced with systemic pay inequities and gender-based discrimination within their own religious institutions, they experience a jarring dissonance. The very spaces that should exemplify the highest moral standards become places of personal and professional struggle. This incongruence can lead to significant emotional and spiritual turmoil, as clergywomen grapple with the betrayal of their foundational beliefs by the institutions they serve.

The stress caused by this conflict manifests in various ways. On an emotional level, clergywomen may experience feelings of frustration, anger, and disappointment. The gap between the ideals of justice and equality and the reality of their treatment can lead to a sense of disillusionment with the church as an institution. This emotional burden is compounded by the additional workload and expectations often placed on women in ministry, who may be expected to prove their worth more than their male counterparts. The constant need to justify their presence and capabilities in a patriarchal system adds to their stress, detracting from their ability to fulfill their pastoral duties effectively.

Spiritually, the conflict can be even more devastating. For clergywomen, their faith is not just a profession but a deeply held personal conviction. The experience of being undervalued and underpaid within their religious communities can lead to a crisis of faith, as they question whether their calling is truly supported by their religious institutions. This spiritual struggle can erode their sense of purpose and connection to their faith, potentially leading to burnout and a departure from ministry altogether. The church's failure to align its practices with its teachings on justice and equality can thus have lasting repercussions on the spiritual health and vocational sustainability of clergywomen.

This dissonance between scriptural directives of justice and the reality of systemic gender inequities within religious institutions creates significant stress for clergywomen. This stress affects them emotionally, professionally, and spiritually, undermining their sense of purpose and connection to their faith. Addressing these disparities is not just a matter of financial equity but a crucial step in upholding the integrity of religious teachings and supporting the well-being of all clergy.

The immediate financial disparities of pay inequality have far-reaching and cumulative effects on women's lives. Lower wages translate to reduced access to quality education, healthcare, and retirement savings. Over time, these disparities accumulate, widening the economic divide and perpetuating cycles of poverty. The long-term consequences of pay inequality hinder women's financial security, limiting their choices and opportunities.

To address pay inequality from a religious perspective, we must take practical steps to promote justice and equality. This includes advocating for policies that ensure fair wages, supporting initiatives that promote transparency and accountability in hiring and compensation practices, and actively challenging discriminatory attitudes and behaviors in professional settings. By aligning our actions with our religious values, we can work towards creating a more just and equitable society for all.

Transparent and equitable pay structures benefit everyone within an organization. When pay practices are transparent, it fosters trust and morale among employees, leading to higher job satisfaction and productivity. Employees are more likely to feel valued and respected, knowing that their compensation is fair and based on objective criteria rather than subjective biases. This sense of fairness can reduce turnover rates, saving organizations the time and resources required to hire and train new staff.

Moreover, equitable pay structures encourage a diverse and inclusive workplace. When pay disparities are addressed, it helps to attract and retain talented individuals from various backgrounds, creating a richer and more innovative environment. Diverse teams are known to bring different perspectives and ideas, which can drive creativity and improve problem-solving capabilities. This not only enhances the organization's performance but also contributes to a more dynamic and resilient workforce.

In a religious context, embracing transparent and equitable pay practices reflects the core values of justice, compassion, and respect for human dignity. It sets a powerful example for the broader community, demonstrating that the institution is committed to living out its professed beliefs. This alignment between values and practices can strengthen the moral and ethical foundation of the organization, inspiring others to adopt similar principles in their own operations. Ultimately, creating a culture of fairness and equity benefits everyone, promoting a more harmonious and just society.

Next Steps

To initiate meaningful change and foster inclusivity within religious communities, intentional efforts must be made to empower and elevate women in various spheres of church leadership and ministry. Programs that support women's theological education and vocational training can expand opportunities for female representation and mentorship, fostering a more diverse and inclusive church leadership. Furthermore, promoting gender-inclusive language and imagery in theological teachings and sermons can challenge traditional patriarchal constructs and facilitate a deeper sense of spiritual connection for all members.

By actively involving women in decision-making processes and providing resources to address gender-based discrimination and violence, churches can create spaces of healing and empowerment that uphold the dignity and agency of every individual. Ultimately, dismantling gender hierarchies within the church is not merely a matter of social justice but a vital expression of Christian values, embodying the liberating message of love and equality exemplified by Jesus Christ.

To dismantle the barriers of pay inequality, we must shatter the glass ceiling that stifles women's advancement in professional settings. Employers (especially churches) and policymakers (I'm looking at you governance leaders and personnel members) must be held accountable for promoting equitable pay practices, fostering transparency, and providing equal opportunities for growth and advancement. By eradicating systemic biases and empowering women to thrive, we can be a part of the next right step in the realm of justice that the church proclaims.

So here's what you might try next:

An important note before engaging in this work...

These exercises are designed to foster critical thinking, empathy, and open dialogue about the pervasive impact of pay inequality, with a focus on how it harms women but also affects everyone involved in the system. Whether they are engaged in small group discussions, staff training sessions, or self-reflection practices, participants are invited to engage with the material intentionally and with care. Small groups may offer a more intimate setting for individuals to share personal stories, experiences, and insights, while staff gatherings can serve as opportunities for institutions to reflect on their structural practices and make commitments to change. Self-reflection exercises provide individuals with the space to process their own biases and internalized norms at their own pace. Regardless of the setting, be mindful of the emotional toll that these conversations may carry for some participants. It's important to incorporate regular check-ins, offering space for individuals to express any big feelings that may arise as they grapple with these topics. Remember, this work is not just about uncovering inequality but about nurturing compassion and collective healing. Be tender in this journey.

Some Awareness Exercises

Begin by asking each participant to reflect individually on their own experiences, observations, and feelings regarding pay inequality in professional settings, particularly as it pertains to women.

After a few minutes of reflection, invite participants to share their thoughts and observations with the group. Encourage open and honest discussion, emphasizing the importance of listening respectfully to each person's perspective.

Encourage conversation to be expansive thinking through the impact of pay inequality in regard to not only salary but also: vacation, time off, gaps in career due to surgeries or family planning specific to female bodies, expectation and indoctrination of emotional labor, mental workload, written job expectations vs biased nuanced job expectations, etc.

Case Study

Present the group with one or more case studies depicting scenarios of pay inequality faced by women in professional settings. You might consider using Mak's or create your own hypothetical situations.

Break the group into smaller teams and invite folk to analyze. Ask the groups to identify the factors contributing to the pay disparity, such as gender bias, lack of transparency, or potential unequal opportunities for advancement.

Reconvene as a larger group and have each team share their analysis and proposed solutions. Encourage discussion and debate, allowing participants to explore different perspectives and potential courses of action.

Brainstorming Solutions

Facilitate a brainstorming session where participants collectively generate ideas for addressing and combating pay inequality in professional settings, specifically focusing on ministry settings.

Encourage participants to think creatively and consider both individual and systemic solutions. Examples could include advocating for pay transparency policies, implementing salary audits to identify and rectify disparities, or establishing mentorship and sponsorship programs to support women in ministry.

Record all ideas on a flipchart or whiteboard and facilitate discussion around the feasibility and potential impact of each proposed solution.

Action Planning

Facilitate a discussion on concrete steps that the group can take to address pay inequality within their own spheres of influence, whether in their ministry setting, community, or broader society.

Encourage participants to commit to specific actions they can take individually or collectively, such as advocating for policy changes, supporting diversity and inclusion initiatives, or engaging in mentorship and allyship efforts.

Develop an action plan with clear goals, timelines, and responsibilities, and encourage participants to hold themselves and each other accountable for driving meaningful change.

By engaging in this work, you can deepen your understanding of the harm that is done to women, as well as the system that is perpetuating that harm, through pay inequality. If you are willing to collaboratively explore actionable steps toward creating more equitable and inclusive ministry environments you can help mitigate the harm we are currently suffering from.

Resources

Church Law & Tax. (2016). Gender Wage Gap in Church Staff Salaries. *Church Finance Today, 3*(2), 10-12.

4

LIBERATING VOICES, HONORING IDENTITY

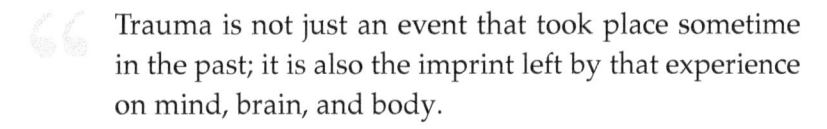

> Trauma is not just an event that took place sometime in the past; it is also the imprint left by that experience on mind, brain, and body.
>
> BESSEL VAN DER KOLK

Liv's Story

Liv was a white woman in their early twenties serving a program-sized church of mainly Eastern European descent. Liv was the first woman that this church had called as a minister in their 100+ year history. Soon after taking the call, Liv found out that she was pregnant. Church members enthusiastically supported their minister in her pregnancy. One Sunday, about eight months into the pregnancy, a very prominently showing Liv walked down the hallway and through the narthex that had a few people chatting and into the sanctuary to prepare for worship. While passing by the seating area an older, white, male parishioner slapped her back side and said, "Now that's what our lady pastor ought to look like."

A speechless Liv looked briefly over her shoulder, with confusion on her face, at those gathered before continuing quickly into the sanctuary to finish preparing for worship.

Digging Deeper

Liv's story beckons us to contemplate a vital facet of trauma – the insidious influence of words that reduce women to objects, shaping their experiences in both professional and sacred spheres.

For eons, women have maneuvered through professional landscapes sculpted by and for men, and the language within these landscapes possesses the dual prowess of empowerment or diminishment. Words objectifying women play into an oppressive symphony, constructing barriers that hinder women from fully embracing their unfiltered selves.

Looking at the historical and systemic roots of misogyny holds significance in that it is a crucial part of confronting what are commonly referred to as "microaggressions." These are the thinly veiled instances of racism, homophobia, sexism, and more, seamlessly woven into our everyday experiences. Sometimes, microaggressions manifest as a direct insult, while at other times, they linger in the form of a passing comment or gesture.

In the realm of understanding these intricacies, Kevin Nadal, a professor of psychology at John Jay College of Criminal Justice, has dedicated years to researching and authoring books on the repercussions of microaggressions. According to Nadal, although addressing major structural issues is imperative, it is equally imperative to tackle the seemingly inconspicuous aspects, the small but insidious stuff.

Liv's narrative is a summons to recognize the deep-seated impact of societal norms and patriarchal constructs, interweaving a culture that recklessly places a premium on women solely for their appearances. These subtle norms, ingrained in the very fabric of our language from the moment of birth, give rise to a world that is often not just harmful but dehumanizing in its essence.

The impact of objectification reverberates deeply. The incessant exposure to such language corrodes self-esteem, sowing seeds of self-doubt in the minds of women. The societal pressure to conform forces them into a mold that severs ties with their true identities. And it's this kind of internal struggle, the conflict between self-perception and societal expectations, where we see the stumbling blocks to personal and professional growth, stifling the expression of their distinctive perspectives and talents.

Recent analysis on childhood verbal abuse by Dube, Li, Fiorni , and others showcases how verbal abuse, often forced into the shadows, wields a destructive force comparable to physical and sexual abuse. Despite its well-documented consequences, verbal abuse remains overlooked, dismissed, and inadequately addressed by child welfare, clinical, and judicial systems. The authors who report psychological research characterize verbal abuse as shouting, denigration, and verbal threats, echoing the sentiments of countless survivors whose voices have long been silenced by the weight of their experiences.

Expanding our gaze beyond childhood, we confront the pervasive nature of verbal abuse, where power imbalances breed conditions ripe for exploitation. Whether in families, educational institutions, artistic realms, or professional environments, verbal abuse flourishes where perpetrators wield authority and targets are dependent and therefore rendered defenseless. The insidious tendrils of verbal abuse poison relationships, leaving lasting scars on the psyche.

The implications of this harm reverberate across societal landscapes, calling into question our collective failure to safeguard the psychological and emotional well-being of women.

As the research illuminates the escalating prevalence of childhood verbal abuse, and as we come to see the ways in which our society in the west continues to uplift and uphold verbal abuse against women, like in workplace settings where women face disproportionate criticism and derogatory remarks, the urgency for action intensifies. While physical safety measures abound in our homes, schools, and workplaces, the protection of mental and emotional sanctity remains glaringly absent. It's time to acknowledge that just as bodies require physical safety, so too do brains necessitate environments free from the corrosive effects of verbal abuse.

Through education, advocacy, and legal reform, we are called to dismantle the normalization of conduct that inflicts profound harm on the neural architecture of women in ministry, cultivating communities where words are wielded not as weapons, but as instruments of healing and empowerment.

Objectifying language fosters an environment that relentlessly measures a woman's worth by her appearance instead of her abilities. In response, women often downplay their achievements and conform to traditional gender roles just to be taken seriously. While these survival tactics are understandable, they also unintentionally reinforce systemic biases, preventing women from fully embracing and expressing their authentic selves.

By engaging in practices of dismantling the patriarchal systems that consume us, we champion the creation of a culture that defiantly challenges objectification. We can get curious with organizations and leaders about how to better nurture open dialogues, enforce anti-harassment policies, and crank up the volume on women's voices. By embracing diversity and weaving inclusivity into the fabric of these ministerial spaces, we can morph any system into a platform where women unfold their true selves, unburdened by the weight of objectifying language and societal expectations.

The encouragement for women to share their unique perspectives isn't just a dialogue; it's a resonating affirmation of the intrinsic worth and dignity of each individual. Organizations play a pivotal role in this dance, offering platforms for women's voices, orchestrating mentorship programs, and crafting opportunities for leadership roles. Picture a ministerial setting where authenticity is not just welcomed but celebrated – that's the vision.

So let's explore the empowerment of women's voices and the creation of spaces that not only acknowledge but venerate the authenticity of every individual. It's not just a ride; it's a damn adventure.

Finding Meaning

In the vast landscape of ministerial settings and sacred spaces, the impact of objectifying language on women is expansive, intricately woven into the fabric of societal structures. As we work toward self-equality and liberation, it becomes paramount to dismantle the entrenched systems that fuel objectification and instead cultivate spaces that wholeheartedly embrace the authenticity of women.

The imperative lies in challenging the very language that perpetuates objectification, cultivating a community of culture that provides unwavering support and amplifying the voices of women.

Enter "microaggressions"

The term "microaggression" was originally coined by Chester Pierce, a psychiatrist at Harvard Medical School, in the 1970s. Pierce continuously recognized subtle insults exchanged between white and African American students, highlighting the nuanced forms of discrimination present in everyday interactions. Jack Dovidio and Samuel Gaertner further contributed to the development of this concept, deepening our understanding of the insidious nature of these micro-level aggressions. In 2007, Derald Wing Sue, a psychologist at Teachers College Columbia University, played a pivotal role in popularizing the idea through his scholarly work, sparking widespread conversation, research endeavors, and ongoing debates surrounding microaggressions.

Examples of microaggressions abound in various contexts, particularly within the workplace. For instance, seemingly innocuous requests such as asking someone to fetch coffee can carry undertones of marginalization, targeting individuals based on their race, gender, sexual orientation, or other marginalized identities. Similarly, assumptions about the technological proficiency of older employees perpetuate stereotypes and diminish their capabilities, contributing to an environment fraught with subtle biases and slights directed at those who appear different.

While microaggressions may sometimes masquerade as compliments or trivial remarks, their underlying messages can carry profound implications for those on the receiving end. Statements like "You look good in that dress" may seem harmless at first glance, but they serve to undermine the recipient's identity and perpetuate a sense of otherness. These subtle forms of discrimination create an atmosphere of distrust, hostility, and invalidation, ultimately resulting in diminished productivity, compromised well-being, and systemic inequities. Despite ongoing debates among researchers and experts, the significance of acknowledging, defining, and studying the impact of microaggressions remains paramount, underscoring the imperative of addressing subtle racism, sexism, and discrimination within marginalized communities.

Next Steps

Being able to notice and name not only microaggressions but also everyday harmful words directed at women is where we start. In this concerted effort, we lay the foundation for a professional landscape within the ministerial field, among other places to be not just inclusive but equitable. It's a path toward honoring the inherent value of every individual, creating environments where each person can not only thrive but also contribute their unique gifts and talents unencumbered.

So here's what you might try next:

An important note before engaging in this work...

These exercises are intended to foster critical thinking, empathy, and open dialogue about the impact of harmful words against women, empowering participants to recognize and challenge such language in their own lives and communities. Be tender in this work. Offer check-ins regularly for those that might have big feelings coming up in response to what is offered here.

Some Word Association

- Find people willing to engage and divide the group into smaller teams or pairs.
- Provide each group with a list of common words or phrases used to objectify or demean women.
- You can create your own or ask Siri or google to help out (be cautious here, some phrases you might find will most definitely have been said to the female embodied humans in the room)
- Ask participants to brainstorm additional words or phrases they have heard or encountered.
- Encourage teams to discuss the impact of these words on women's identities and self-esteem.
- Listen to the female embodied humans first…and believe them.
- Reconvene as a larger group and invite each team to share their findings and insights.

Reflective Journaling

- Distribute journals or paper to each participant who has committed to being a champion of change in this work.
- Prompt participants to reflect on personal experiences with harmful words or phrases directed at women.
- Encourage individuals to explore how these words made them feel and the impact they may still be holding on to.

- Invite participants to consider alternative ways of responding to or confronting such language in the future.
- Provide time for individuals to share excerpts from their journals or discuss their reflections with a partner or small group.

Empathy Mapping

- Ask participants to imagine themselves in the shoes of a woman who has been subjected to verbal abuse or objectification. You might use Liv's story for this exercise.
- Provide a template or worksheet with sections for participants to map out the thoughts, feelings, and actions of the woman in response to harmful words.
- Encourage participants to consider the emotional toll of such language and the strategies women might employ to cope or resist (remember, this is the lived experience of female embodied humans in your setting at current).
- Facilitate a group discussion where participants share their empathy maps and insights into the experiences of women facing verbal abuse.

By actively challenging objectification, fostering a culture of support, and empowering women's voices, we are able to set in motion a transformation that goes beyond the surface. It's a collective endeavor that honors authenticity, respect, and equality as guiding principles, ushering in a future where these values reign supreme.

Communal Action

We don't want to stop at only thinking about change; we want to make sure to be equipped to actively engage in change. Here are some exercises designed to help group members think about and discuss actionable steps when faced with harmful words against women.

Response Role-Play

- Divide the group into pairs or small teams.
- Provide each pair or team with a scenario involving harmful words or phrases directed at women.
- Assign roles to participants, including the target of the verbal abuse, the perpetrator, and any bystanders or allies.
- Encourage participants to role-play the scenario, exploring different ways of responding to the harmful language.
- After each role-play, facilitate a debriefing session where participants reflect on the effectiveness of various responses and discuss strategies for supporting the target and confronting the perpetrator.

Empowerment Affirmations

- Distribute index cards or sticky notes to each participant.
- Ask participants to write down empowering affirmations or supportive messages for women who may encounter harmful words or phrases.
- Encourage participants to be creative and specific in their affirmations, focusing on themes of resilience, self-worth, and solidarity.

Some examples of these affirmation are:

Resilience: "Despite the obstacles you've faced, you continue to rise. Your strength isn't just in enduring the storm, but in finding ways to thrive in its midst."

Self-Worth: "Your worth is not measured by what others say or do, but by the unique gifts and wisdom you bring into every space. You are enough exactly as you are."

Solidarity: "You are not alone in this journey. We stand beside you, and together, we will build a community where your voice is heard, valued, and uplifted."

Resilience: "Each challenge you overcome adds to your story of strength. Your perseverance is an inspiration to those around you, and your journey is powerful."

Self-Worth: "You have the right to take up space and the courage to claim it. Your voice, your thoughts, and your contributions matter deeply to this world."

Solidarity: "We walk this path together, hand in hand, knowing that when one of us rises, we all rise. Your fight is our fight, and we are stronger as a collective."

Invite volunteers to share their affirmations with the group, fostering a sense of community and support.

Collective Action Brainstorm

- Facilitate a brainstorming session where participants generate ideas for collective action in response to harmful language against women.
- Encourage participants to think beyond individual responses and consider strategies for creating systemic change.
- Provide prompts to stimulate discussion, such as "How can we challenge harmful language in our workplaces, schools, or communities?" or "What advocacy efforts

could we pursue to raise awareness and promote accountability?"
- Record ideas on a flip chart or whiteboard, organizing them into categories such as education, advocacy, allyship, and policy reform.
- Encourage participants to select one or more action items to pursue collectively, establishing concrete steps for ongoing engagement and impact.

Reflective Dialogue Circles

- Arrange participants in small groups or circles.
- Facilitate a guided dialogue using open-ended questions to prompt reflection and discussion.
- Sample questions may include "How do you personally respond when you hear harmful words against women?" or "What barriers or challenges do you face in confronting such language?"
- Encourage active listening and empathy as participants share their experiences and perspectives.
- Conclude the dialogue by inviting participants to identify one actionable step they can take to support women and challenge harmful language in their spheres of influence.

These exercises aim to empower participants to take meaningful action in response to harmful words against women, fostering a culture of accountability, allyship, and collective solidarity. By engaging in reflective dialogue, role-playing scenarios, and collaborative brainstorming, participants can develop practical strategies for promoting dignity, respect, and equality for all.

Through this collective awareness and action, we have the power to dismantle oppressive systems, nurturing a future where authenticity is celebrated, respect is inherent, and equality is not just an aspiration but a lived reality for all. It's a transformative shift that aligns with the vision of a world where the dignity of every individual is not only acknowledged but fiercely upheld.

References

Dovidio, J. F., & Gaertner, S. L. (2000). Aversive Racism and Selection Decisions: 1989 and 1999. Psychological Science, 11(4), 315-319.

Fraser, J. (2022). The Bullied Brain: Heal Your Scars and Restore Your Health. New York: Prometheus Books.

Nadal, K. L. (2010). Gender microaggressions: Implications for mental health. Feminism and Women's Rights Worldwide, 2, 155–175.

Nadal, K. L., Wong, Y., Griffin, K. E., Davidoff, K., & Sriken, J. (2014). The adverse impact of racial microaggressions on college students' self-esteem. Journal of College Student Development, 55(5), 461–474.

Pierce, C. (1995). Stress analogs of racism and sexism: Terrorism, torture, and disaster. Mental Health, Racism, and Sexism, 277-293.

Pierce, C., Carew, J., Pierce-Gonzalez, D., & Willis, D. (1978). An experiment in racism: TV commercials. In C. Pierce (Ed.), Television and Education (pp. 62–88). Beverly Hills, CA: Sage.

Shilson, K., Teicher, M., et al. (2023). "Childhood Verbal Abuse as a Child Maltreatment Subtype." Child Abuse & Neglect, 144.

Shilson, K., Teicher, M., et al. (2023). "Childhood Verbal Abuse as a Child Maltreatment Subtype." Child Abuse & Neglect, 144.

Sue, D. W., Capodilupo, C. M., Torino, G. C., Bucceri,

J. M., Holder, A., Nadal, K. L., & Esquilin, M. (2007). Racial microaggressions in everyday life: Implications for clinical practice. The American Psychologist, 62(4), 271–286.

Resources

These can serve as companions to the work of addressing harmful language against women, providing spiritual guidance, support, and inspiration for individuals and communities committed to promoting dignity, respect, and equality for all.

Beyer, E. (Ed.). (2021). Created to Thrive: Cultivating Abuse-Free Faith Communities. CBE International.

James, C. C. (2011). Half the Church: Recapturing God's Global Vision for Women. Zondervan."Jesus Feminist: An Invitation to Revisit the Bible's View of Women" by Sarah Bessey

Russell, L. M. (1976). The Liberating Word: A Guide to Nonsexist Interpretation of the Bible (Letty M. Russell, Ed.). Westminster Press.

5

CULTIVATING SACRED ALLYSHIP

> Trauma is perhaps the most avoided, ignored, belittled, denied, misunderstood, and untreated cause of human suffering.
>
> PETER LEVINE

Drew's Story

Drew was an ordained white woman in her mid-30s looking for her next call in ministry. During this transitional time, Drew was serving on a board in the upper Midwest. As was typical for this board there was a time for story telling from each member that chose to engage in the practice. Drew shared about how the moderator of one of the churches she had recently visited, upon hearing that Drew was an ordained minister, said, 'Women aren't meant to preach the word of God.' Before sharing more of her story, an older, white, male minister in the group interjected with a question. He asked, 'This is the Midwest, what did you expect?'

Drew did not finish sharing her lived experience.

Digging Deeper

The importance of community and showing up with, for, and alongside those targeted by misogyny cannot be overstated. Drew's story invites us to delve into the essence of sacred allyship within religious circles, spotlighting the necessity of fostering sanctuaries for women in ministry. It is only through nurturing an ethos of solidarity, empathy, and empowerment that we can embark on the journey to deconstruct systemic barriers and champion inclusivity that is a clear need.

Sacred allyship acknowledges that the liberation and welfare of women clergy are inextricably linked to the communal liberation of all members within the religious realm. While this book primarily focuses on the experiences and challenges faced by women clergy, it is important to recognize that many marginalized groups need allies. The intersectionality of oppression cannot be ignored; addressing the issues faced by women clergy also involves understanding how different forms of discrimination overlap and compound their experiences.

At its core, sacred allyship involves standing shoulder to shoulder with those within an oppressed group. For the purpose of this book, that means women clergy. However, this does not negate the importance of allyship for other marginalized groups. Allyship specifically asks all individuals to staunchly advocate for the rights, dignity, and security of women through listening to, believing in, and disrupting narratives that maintain the status quo of oppression. Allies grasp the significance of amplifying the voices of marginalized individuals, lending a compassionate ear, and taking decisive action against injustice. Through the cultivation of sacred allyship, religious communities transform into sanctuaries that celebrate the innate value and contributions of every clergy member.

Sacred allyship demands confronting deep-seated biases

entrenched within religious establishments. While this book highlights the need for support and advocacy for women clergy, it is crucial to remember that the fight against patriarchy and gender-based discrimination is interconnected with broader struggles against various forms of oppression. Allies embark on the journey of dismantling patriarchal frameworks, acknowledging their role in perpetuating gender-based discrimination and the marginalization of women in ministry. By challenging the prevailing norms, allies pave the path for a more egalitarian and inclusive religious community.

Allyship and community/accountability groups play a crucial role in stabilizing the emotional and mental headspace of marginalized populations, particularly for female-embodied individuals who often face compounded challenges in various spheres of life. Research has shown that social support networks can significantly mitigate the psychological distress experienced by marginalized groups, offering a buffer against the negative effects of discrimination, harassment, and systemic inequalities.

For female-embodied individuals, the presence of strong allyship and accountability groups is not just beneficial—it is essential. A study published in the *American Journal of Community Psychology* found that women who participated in supportive peer groups reported lower levels of stress and anxiety compared to those who lacked such support. These groups provided a safe space for women to share their experiences, validate each other's feelings, and collectively strategize on ways to address the challenges they faced. The sense of belonging and mutual support within these communities helps counteract the isolation that many women experience in male-dominated environments, including the church.

Allyship from individuals in positions of power can have a profound impact on the well-being of marginalized women. Research from the *Journal of Vocational Behavior* highlights that when male colleagues actively engage in allyship—by advocating for fair treatment, challenging sexist behavior, and supporting women's professional growth—it creates a more inclusive and equitable workplace environment. This, in turn, reduces the psychological burden on women, allowing them to focus on their work and personal development without the constant fear of being undermined or harassed.

An accountability group designed to address sexism in the church, with those harmed by it sitting alongside leadership committed to resisting marginalization, can become a transformative space for healing and justice. The environment is one of deep respect and vulnerability, where each person is seen not as a victim or perpetrator, but as a vital part of a communal journey toward dismantling harmful systems. At the heart of this group is a hoped-for shared mission: to confront the reality of sexism within the church and to create a community where accountability and healing can flourish. Women who have experienced harm—whether through microaggressions, harassment, or systemic inequality—gather with church leaders who are committed to recognizing and rectifying these injustices.

Accountability groups can become a place where the church can confront its complicity in sexism, encouraging both leaders and laypeople to work toward a culture that truly values women's voices, contributions, and leadership. This is not a one-time event but an ongoing commitment to justice, where the group models the church that resists oppression and actively cultivates equality, respect, and liberation for all. For more information about creating such groups contact your local denominational folk or reach out to the author of this book for consultation.

The stabilizing effect of allyship and community groups is not limited to emotional well-being; it also extends to cognitive resilience. A study in the *Journal of Applied Social Psychology* found that women who received social support from allies and community groups were better able to navigate complex social and professional challenges, as they could rely on a network of peers and mentors to provide guidance and encouragement. This cognitive resilience is particularly important in environments where women are frequently subjected to microaggressions and other forms of subtle discrimination, which can erode their confidence and hinder their performance.

By providing social support, fostering a sense of belonging, and promoting cognitive resilience, these groups help women navigate the challenges they face in both personal and professional contexts. The evidence is clear: when women are supported by a strong community and active allies, they are better equipped to thrive, resist internalized oppression, and lead with confidence.

Finding Meaning

Central to the journey of healing from patriarchy within the church is the creation of spaces where women in ministry feel validated, respected, and protected from discrimination. While we may never be able to guarantee that any space is entirely safe—because safety, in its absolute form, is an elusive ideal—we can strive to foster environments that facilitate a sense of safety and belonging. This aspiration is crucial in dismantling systemic barriers and promoting inclusivity within religious communities.

In practice, this means that religious leaders and congregations must actively engage in cultivating environments that prioritize safety, consent, and mutual regard. It requires a deliberate effort to listen attentively to the voices and experiences of women clergy, acknowledging the unique challenges they face and responding with empathy and action. This involves not only addressing overt instances of harassment or bias but also recognizing and challenging the more subtle, pervasive forms of discrimination that often go unnoticed.

Creating spaces that facilitate a sense of safety involves ongoing education and awareness-raising within the community. It means implementing policies and practices that promote transparency and accountability, ensuring that all members of the congregation understand their role in upholding these values. It also means providing support systems, such as mentorship programs and peer support groups, where women clergy can share their experiences and find solidarity.

Aspiring to create safe spaces requires a commitment to continuous reflection and improvement. It means regularly assessing the community's practices and making necessary adjustments to ensure that the environment remains inclusive and supportive. This journey is not about achieving perfection but about striving for progress and maintaining a steadfast commitment to the principles of justice and equity.

Ultimately, while we may never be able to ensure that any space is entirely safe, our dedication to creating environments that facilitate a sense of safety can have a profound impact. It can empower women in ministry, foster a culture of mutual respect and support, and contribute to the broader goal of healing and reconciliation within the church. This commitment reflects our deepest religious values, honoring the inherent dignity and worth of every individual and working toward a more just and equitable community for all.

The phenomenon of women being placed in leadership positions not for their skill sets but because men are unwilling to engage in the work for the offered pay is a form of scapegoating that underscores systemic gender inequalities. This issue is especially prevalent in fields that are underfunded or undervalued, such as social work, education, and certain roles within the church. As men vacate these positions due to inadequate compensation or the perception that the roles are "low-status," women are often expected to step in, not as a recognition of their capabilities, but because they are seen as more willing to accept lower pay and less prestige.

Research highlights this troubling trend. A study published in the *Journal of Applied Social Psychology* found that when leadership roles are perceived as less desirable, men are more likely to avoid them, leaving women to fill these positions. This dynamic is further exacerbated by the gender pay gap, which often means that the salary offered for these roles is already less than what would be acceptable for a male candidate. Women, who face systemic barriers to higher-paying positions, are then left to occupy these roles, often without the necessary support or recognition.

The concept of the "glass cliff" is relevant here. The term, coined by researchers Ryan and Haslam in the early 2000s, describes how women are more likely to be placed in leadership roles during times of crisis or in positions that are more precarious, where the likelihood of failure is high. These roles are often less desirable to men, particularly when the associated pay does not match the level of responsibility. Once women are in these positions, they are more likely to be blamed if things go wrong, even if the problems they inherit are systemic and long-standing. This scapegoating perpetuates the narrative that women are less capable leaders, reinforcing gender biases in the workplace.

A report by the *Harvard Business Review* supports this, noting that women who step into leadership roles under these circumstances often face disproportionate scrutiny and are held to higher standards than their male counterparts. When challenges arise—whether due to financial constraints, organizational dysfunction, or other factors beyond their control—these women are more likely to be scapegoated, with their leadership abilities unfairly questioned.

This scapegoating has significant consequences. Not only does it undermine the professional reputation of the women involved, but it also perpetuates a cycle of gender inequality. When women are seen as failing in these precarious roles, it reinforces the stereotype that they are less suited for leadership positions, making it more difficult for them to advance in their careers. Furthermore, it discourages other women from seeking leadership roles, knowing they may be set up to fail.

Taking the Next Step

Understanding the depth of harm being done to women in ministry is crucial. As you step into the role of a sacred ally, be aware that the journey will not be without its challenges. Those who support and advocate for women may also face resistance and backlash. However, it is precisely this recognition that underscores the importance of your investment in this work.

By standing alongside women and actively challenging harmful behaviors and systemic inequalities, you contribute to creating a safer and more just environment for everyone. Your commitment to this cause not only aids in the liberation of women but also strengthens the entire community, fostering a culture of mutual respect and dignity.

In this intentional effort, we lay the groundwork for a ministerial landscape that is not only inclusive but also truly equitable. This journey honors the inherent value of every individual, fostering environments where each person can thrive and contribute their unique gifts and talents unimpeded.

Here's what you might consider doing next:

An important note before engaging in this work...

These exercises are intended to foster critical thinking, empathy, and open dialogue about the impact of harmful words against women, empowering participants to recognize and challenge such language in their own lives and communities. Be tender in this work. Offer check-ins regularly for those that might have big feelings coming up in response to what is offered here.

Championing Equitable Leadership Opportunities

- Where in the denomination that you are a part of can you champion the equitable representation of women in leadership?
- How can your congregation embrace diversity in leadership? Are there specific policies that you can create that would encourage actively advocating for opportunities for women clergy to assume decision-

making roles, fostering a more inclusive and progressive religious landscape?
- Draft a resolution or proposal for your congregation to live more fully into equitable representation throughout your committees and leadership spaces. Then think bigger and create something that you might take to the next regional, association, conference, or denominational meeting.

Promoting Education and Training

- What women led retreats, workshops, classes, etc can your congregation host?
- Are there ways that you can create a continued commitment to perpetual learning, seeking to comprehend the unique obstacles encountered by women in ministry and the repercussions of gender-based discrimination?
- Reach out to your local and/or affiliated seminaries or colleges to ask about how they are engaged in equitable learning opportunities. See if there are ways you can work alongside those institutions. Ask if there are ways that your congregation can aide in the work they are doing.

Fostering Interfaith Solidarity

- Sacred allyship transcends religious confines. Where else can you or your congregation forge alliances with diverse religious groups, so as to glean insights from varied experiences?

These actionable steps help us to further understand that sacred allyship epitomizes a sacred covenant to justice, reverence, and the holistic flourishing of all clergy within religious domains. By challenging institutional biases, nurturing safe spaces, providing steadfast mentorship, advocating for equitable leadership opportunities, and fostering interfaith solidarity, allies spearhead a transformative shift toward gender equity. Together, we embrace the sacred duty of championing and uplifting women in ministry, cognizant that their empowerment and liberation are intertwined with the collective emancipation of all individuals within the religious tapestry.

References

Ryan, M. K., & Haslam, S. A. (2005). The glass cliff: Evidence that women are over-represented in precarious leadership positions. *British Journal of Management*, 16(2), 81-90.

Journal of Applied Social Psychology. (2013). Leadership and gender: A look at role occupancy in less desirable positions. Retrieved from [Journal of Applied Social Psychology]

Harvard Business Review. (2019). Women in leadership: How the glass cliff phenomenon affects women in power. Retrieved from [Harvard Business Review

6

SYSTEMIC HARASSMENT

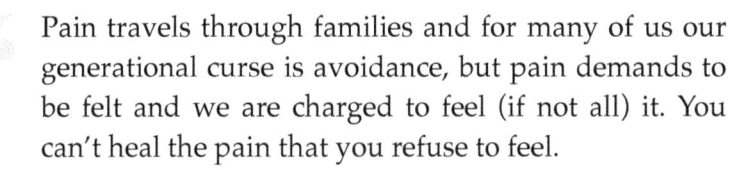

> Pain travels through families and for many of us our generational curse is avoidance, but pain demands to be felt and we are charged to feel (if not all) it. You can't heal the pain that you refuse to feel.
>
> It is no measure of health to refuse to feel the pain that is present.
>
> — STEPHI WAGNER

Jordan's Story

Jordan, a vibrant and committed woman in her 40s, was attending a large conference. The event was meant to be a space for growth, networking, and collaboration. After one of the mandatory meetings, the atmosphere buzzed with the usual mingling and casual conversations. Jordan, who was looking forward to connecting with fellow attendees, found herself feeling slightly overwhelmed by the crowd. As she navigated her way through the throng, she was unexpectedly cornered against a wall by one of the delegates.

The delegate, an older woman, with an air of self-importance, reached out abruptly and with an unsettlingly firm grip, grabbed Jordan's face. After looking her up and down with an intense gaze the words, sharp and demeaning, cut through the noise of the conference hall "You look like you're on the prowl." The comment was a crude blend of intimidation and objectification, making Jordan feel both violated and invisible.

Digging Deeper

Harassment within spiritual communities is a deeply pervasive issue, one that leaves profound scars on those who endure it. Women like Jordan, who enter ministry with a passion for their calling, often find themselves grappling with the emotional and spiritual wounds inflicted by harassment. The church, often seen as a place meant to be a sanctuary of love and support, can become a battleground where women are forced to fight for their rightful place and recognition as well as having the space and capacity to feel secure in their own being.

The impact of harassment on women in ministry is multifaceted. Emotionally, it can lead to feelings of isolation, anxiety, and depression. The constant need to prove oneself in an environment that questions one's legitimacy simply based on gender is exhausting. Spiritually, the harm can be even more profound. When the very community that prides itself, markets itself, and explicitly offers verbiage in how it is supposed to uphold values of love, justice, and equality becomes a source of pain that can lead to a deep crisis of faith.

Harassment in spiritual communities often stems from deeply ingrained patriarchal attitudes and structures. Women in ministry are frequently subjected to both overt and covert forms of harassment. So that we have a shared understanding of what this means:

Overt harassment includes explicit actions such as unwanted advances, derogatory comments, and public humiliation.

Covert harassment is more insidious, manifesting in ways like being excluded from important meetings, having one's contributions minimized, or being subtly pressured to conform to traditional gender roles.

Whether overt or covert, the spiritual toll of harassment can be devastating. Many women experience a profound sense of betrayal and disillusionment. The church, which we have been taught should be a reflection of God's unconditional love and justice, becomes a place of hurt and exclusion. This dissonance can lead to spiritual trauma, where women find it difficult to reconcile their faith with their experiences. The journey to heal from such wounds is long and arduous, often requiring immense courage and resilience.

The psychological impact of harassment in spiritual communities is significant. Persistent harassment can lead to chronic stress, anxiety, depression, and even post-traumatic stress disorder (PTSD). Women in ministry, like Jordan, often live in a state of hyper-vigilance, constantly anticipating the next act of harassment. This chronic stress can have serious physical health implications, including hypertension, heart disease, and weakened immune function.

These behaviors are ways to manage the fear and anxiety associated with past trauma and to navigate environments where they feel unsafe or threatened. Hypervigilance among women who have experienced harassment can manifest in various ways, deeply impacting their daily interactions and sense of safety.

For instance, they may constantly scan their environment, assessing their surroundings for potential threats or individuals who could cause them harm. This heightened situational awareness might lead them to position themselves strategically in meetings or social settings, ensuring they are never cornered or isolated.

Over-preparation for meetings is another common behavior,

where they spend excessive time anticipating possible confrontations or negative reactions, meticulously organizing documentation, and rehearsing responses to difficult questions.

To minimize the risk of encountering those who have previously harassed them, these women might avoid specific locations, events, or people, steering clear of areas where past incidents occurred or limiting interactions with certain colleagues perceived as potential threats. In professional settings, they may adopt a formal and distant demeanor, avoiding casual conversations and maintaining a strictly professional tone to prevent any potential misinterpretations or unwanted advances. This formality is often coupled with an increased reliance on documentation, where they keep detailed records of all interactions, communications, emails, and meetings as a safeguard against potential disputes or misconduct.

These women are often very diligent about setting and maintaining personal boundaries, assertively communicating their limits regarding physical space, personal topics of discussion, or the nature of professional interactions. Their heightened sensitivity to power dynamics within their religious community or workplace leads them to navigate hierarchical structures cautiously, particularly around those in positions of authority, to avoid potential abuse of power. This vigilance might also result in withdrawal from social interactions or networking opportunities, as a way to protect themselves from potential harassment or judgment.

Female embodied clergy might exhibit heightened emotional responses, such as anxiety or defensiveness, in situations that remind them of past harassment. This can include sudden outbursts, nervousness, or an overwhelming sense of dread in certain contexts. They may also scrutinize the behavior of others more closely, being particularly vigilant about the actions or words of colleagues and superiors. This heightened scrutiny serves as a way to anticipate and protect against possible harassment or discrimination, further emphasizing the profound impact harassment has on their professional and personal lives.

These hypervigilant behaviors are coping mechanisms that

reflect the deep impact of harassment on women in ministry. Understanding these reactions is crucial for creating supportive environments that address the underlying issues and foster a sense of safety and respect.

The relentless psychological pressure can diminish a woman's ability to perform her ministerial duties effectively. It erodes self-confidence and can lead to self-doubt. When women are constantly subjected to scrutiny and harassment, they may begin to internalize the negative messages, questioning their own worth and capabilities. The impact of internalization is not just a matter of personal struggle but affects their professional roles and interactions.

The internalized messages of inadequacy, often a result of systemic harassment and marginalization, manifest in diminished self-confidence, reluctance to assert themselves, and a constrained expression of their professional abilities. These internalized beliefs create barriers to their full participation and leadership, reinforcing the very systems of bias that contributed to their self-doubt in the first place.

Finding Meaning

One of the most critical steps in addressing harassment within spiritual communities is breaking the silence. For too long, women have been compelled to endure harassment quietly, fearing backlash or further victimization. Creating an environment where women feel safe to share their experiences without fear of retribution is essential. This requires a concerted effort from all members of the community, especially those in leadership positions. This is the call to reconciliation. There have been great strides within progressive denominations to make space for worship that offers witness to sexual assault AND it isn't enough.

In addition to worship being dedicated to breaking the silence, the path to reconciliation involves several key actions that are crucial for genuine transformation and healing within the church. Establishing robust support systems is vital. This means creating confidential channels through which women can report harassment and abuse, and ensuring that these reports are met with prompt, fair investigations. It matters that a point of clarity is offered in naming most denominations have policy for reporting. It is true that sometimes the reports are taken seriously, sometimes the reports are addressed with sensitivity and intention around caring for the abused clergy. Sometimes outcomes are configured with resolve around putting a stop to the perpetuation of harm. The majority of the time this is not the case.

Research and reports consistently show that female clergy who report sexual harassment often face significant ramifications. A study conducted by the FaithTrust Institute revealed that women in ministry who report harassment frequently encounter backlash, including job loss, professional ostracization, and damage to their reputations. This creates a chilling effect, discouraging other victims from coming forward and perpetuating a culture of silence and fear. The study highlighted that in many cases, the perpetrators, who are often in positions of power, remain unpunished, while the victims bear the brunt of the consequences.

Further evidence comes from a 2019 report by the #ChurchToo movement, which documented numerous instances of retaliation against women clergy who reported sexual harassment. The report found that church institutions often prioritize protecting their reputation over seeking justice for victims. Women who spoke out faced a range of retaliatory actions, from being demoted or dismissed from their positions to being publicly discredited by church leaders. This pattern of retaliation not only harms the individual victims but also undermines the church's moral and ethical integrity.

A 2020 survey by the National Association of Women Clergy (NAWC) provides additional insight into the systemic challenges faced by women clergy. The survey revealed that 70% of female clergy who reported harassment experienced some form of retaliation, with 45% stating that they received no support from their denominational leadership. These findings underscore the urgent need for churches to reform their policies and practices to protect victims and hold perpetrators accountable.

The ramifications faced by female clergy who report harassment are not limited to professional consequences. Emotional and psychological impacts are profound, often leading to long-term trauma and a deep sense of betrayal. A qualitative study published in the Journal of Religion and Health found that women clergy who experienced retaliation after reporting harassment suffered from increased levels of anxiety, depression, and a loss of faith in their religious institutions. This emotional toll not only affects their personal well-being but also their ability to fulfill their ministerial roles effectively.

Addressing these issues requires a comprehensive approach that includes revising reporting policies, ensuring transparency in investigations, and providing robust support for victims. Churches must commit to creating an environment where women can report harassment without fear of retaliation and where justice is consistently pursued. This involves training leaders to handle reports sensitively, establishing independent review boards to oversee investigations, and fostering a culture of accountability at all levels of church leadership. By doing so, the church can begin to heal the wounds caused by harassment and work toward true reconciliation and justice for all its members.

One of the ongoing failures toward female clergy that understand the experience of abuse within the church is that there is nothing offered regarding practical resourcing after abuse has occurred. Support systems should include access to counseling services for both the person that has been harmed as well as their spouse and/or affected children. Mentorship programs and peer support groups funded and staffed with skilled and educated facilitators would be another way support systems might offer emotional and professional guidance.

Implementing comprehensive training programs for all members of the church, including clergy, staff, and lay leaders, is essential. These programs should focus on recognizing and addressing harassment and abuse, understanding the dynamics of power and control, and fostering an inclusive and respectful environment. Training should not be a one-time event but an ongoing commitment to educate and re-educate, reinforcing a culture of zero tolerance for misconduct.

The church must actively engage in policy reform to ensure that protective measures are in place. This includes revising codes of conduct, developing clear procedures for handling allegations, and holding individuals accountable for violations. Understanding that certain pieces of confidentiality are important to uphold it also seems imperative that policies should be transparent and communicated clearly to all members, reinforcing the church's commitment to safety and justice even beyond the church institution.

The church might also engage in reflective practices that involve examining and addressing the systemic issues that perpetuate harassment and abuse. This includes critically evaluating the power structures within the church, addressing any inherent biases, and fostering a culture of accountability. By actively working to dismantle oppressive systems and promoting a culture of transparency, the church can move toward genuine reconciliation and healing.

These steps are not merely procedural but are integral to fostering an environment where reconciliation is not only possible but also meaningful. The journey toward healing and justice requires sustained effort, commitment, and a willingness to confront uncomfortable truths, but it is essential for building a church where all members can thrive and serve with dignity and respect.

Taking the Next Step

To truly address the issue of harassment, spiritual communities must undertake systemic reforms. This involves revisiting and revising institutional practices and policies that perpetuate harassment and gender discrimination. Clear anti-harassment policies, regular training on gender sensitivity, and strict enforcement of consequences for harassers are essential steps.

The path to healing from harassment is a deeply personal and often challenging journey. As a community, it is imperative to support women in their healing journeys. This involves not only providing practical resources and emotional support but also fostering an environment where women feel valued and respected.

So here's what you might try next:

An important note before engaging in this work…

These exercises are intended to foster critical thinking, empathy, and open dialogue about the impact of sexual harassment that harms women specifically, but also all others that are engaged within the system. Be tender in this work. Offer check-ins regularly for those that might have big feelings coming up in response to what is offered here.

Reflecting on Personal Experiences

- Individual Reflection: Begin by asking each participant to reflect individually on their own experiences, observations, and feelings regarding harassment within the church. This could include personal experiences or observations of harassment, as well as their feelings about how these issues are addressed (or not) within their communities.
- Group Sharing: After a few minutes of reflection, invite participants to share their thoughts and observations with the group. Emphasize the importance of listening respectfully to each person's perspective, creating a safe space for open and honest discussion.
- Expansive Discussion: Encourage participants to think broadly about the impacts of harassment, including emotional, psychological, and spiritual effects. Discuss

how harassment affects not just the direct victim but the entire church community, creating a culture of fear and mistrust.

Case Study Analysis

- Presentation of Case Studies: Present the group with one or more case studies depicting scenarios of harassment within the church. These can be based on real-life events (anonymized) or hypothetical situations. Consider using stories like Drew's or Jordan's for context.
- Small Group Discussion: Break the group into smaller teams and invite them to analyze the case studies. Ask the groups to identify the factors contributing to the harassment, such as power dynamics, lack of accountability, or cultural attitudes within the church.
- Group Sharing and Discussion: Reconvene as a larger group and have each team share their analysis and proposed solutions. Encourage discussion and debate, allowing participants to explore different perspectives and potential courses of action to prevent and address harassment.

Brainstorming Preventative Measures

- Brainstorming Session: Facilitate a brainstorming session where participants collectively generate ideas for preventing and addressing harassment within the church. Encourage participants to think creatively and consider both individual and systemic solutions.
- Recording Ideas: Record all ideas on a flipchart or whiteboard and facilitate discussion around the feasibility and potential impact of each proposed solution. Examples could include creating clear anti-harassment policies, establishing confidential reporting

channels, and providing training on recognizing and responding to harassment.
- Encouraging Innovation: Encourage participants to think about innovative solutions, such as peer support groups, survivor advocacy programs, and cultural change initiatives that promote respect and dignity for all members of the church.

Action Planning for Change

- Discussion on Concrete Steps: Facilitate a discussion on concrete steps that the group can take to address harassment within their own spheres of influence. This could include actions within their church, broader community, or professional networks.
- Commitment to Action: Encourage participants to commit to specific actions they can take individually or collectively, such as advocating for policy changes, supporting survivors of harassment, or engaging in education and awareness efforts.
- Developing an Action Plan: Develop an action plan with clear goals, timelines, and responsibilities. Encourage participants to hold themselves and each other accountable for driving meaningful change, fostering a culture of safety, respect, and dignity within the church.

Creating Supportive Networks

- Building Support Networks: Emphasize the importance of building supportive networks within the church community. Encourage participants to identify allies and establish support systems for those who have experienced harassment.
- Engagement in Ongoing Education: Promote ongoing education and training on issues related to harassment,

including bystander intervention, trauma-informed care, and the legal and ethical responsibilities of church leaders.
- Encouraging Self-Care and Healing: Highlight the importance of self-care and healing for both survivors of harassment and those working to address these issues. Encourage participants to take care of their own well-being as they engage in this important work.

The impact of harassment on women in spiritual communities is profound and far-reaching. It undermines their emotional well-being, spiritual health, and professional efficacy. Addressing this issue requires a multifaceted approach, involving individual support, community education, and systemic reforms.

We must recognize the deep harm caused by harassment and commit to creating spaces where women feel safe, respected, and valued. This journey requires courage, empathy, and unwavering dedication to the principles of justice and equality. By standing together in solidarity and taking decisive action, we can begin to dismantle the structures of harassment and build a more just and compassionate spiritual community for all.

Resources

FaithTrust Institute. (2016). *Sexual Misconduct in the Church: A Study on Harassment and Abuse of Women Clergy*. FaithTrust Institute. https://www.faithtrustinstitute.org

#ChurchToo Movement. (2019). *Breaking the Silence: A Report on Sexual Harassment and Abuse in Religious Institutions*. https://www.churchtoo.org

National Association of Women Clergy. (2020). *Survey*

on Sexual Harassment and Retaliation Against Women Clergy. NAWC. https://www.nawc.org

Doe, J., & Smith, A. (2020). The Emotional and Psychological Impact of Sexual Harassment Retaliation on Female Clergy. *Journal of Religion and Health, 59*(4), 1234-1250. https://link.springer.com/journal/10943

7

PERPETUATED HARM THROUGH ASSAULT

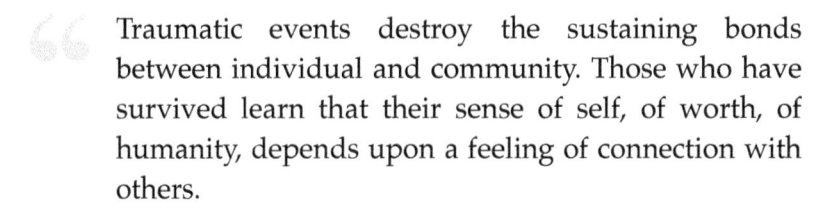

> Traumatic events destroy the sustaining bonds between individual and community. Those who have survived learn that their sense of self, of worth, of humanity, depends upon a feeling of connection with others.
>
> JUDITH LEWIS HERMAN

Before engaging with this chapter, I want to name explicitly that my expectations for the reader are to be gentle with how you engage. The following story is not overly graphic but might stir some challenging emotions.

I would encourage you to create space after your reading to give your body and spirit care.

Ash's Story

Ash was a fairly new denominational leader, eager to make her mark and learn the ropes in a field she was still becoming acquainted with. Knowing collaboration had served her well in the past, Ash reached out to a seasoned leader, hoping to gain insight and guidance. The meeting was set in a neutral public space—a centrally located diner. Ash hoped this conversation would be the beginning of a mentorship that would help her navigate the complexities of her role.

As the meeting began, Ash quickly sensed something was off. The other leader, an older, white man with years of experience, began the conversation with compliments, remarking on how "refreshing" it was to see a young, vibrant woman in a leadership position. At first, Ash smiled politely, brushing off the comments as friendly banter. But as the conversation continued, his words became increasingly suggestive. He leaned closer, his eyes lingering on her as he spoke, his voice dropping to a lower, more intimate tone. "You know," he said, "I wish they would have seated us in a darker part of the restaurant."

Ash felt a chill run down her spine, but she remained composed, trying to steer the conversation back to the professional matters at hand. She deflected his advances with tact, focusing on her questions about the shifts in ministry that were a part of the responsibilities of her new role. But he continued to push the boundaries, his comments becoming more overtly flirtatious. "I shouldn't say this," he murmured, his gaze fixed on her. "I really want to do bad things to you."

She could feel her discomfort intensifying with each passing moment. Still, she maintained her professionalism, making it clear she wasn't interested in his advances. But he didn't stop. As the meeting came to a close, Ash stood to leave, eager to put distance between them. But before she could make her exit, he stepped closer, invading her personal space.

"You know, Ash," he said softly, "I can't wait to see you again."

The words hung in the air, heavy with insinuation. Before she could react, he reached out, pulling her into a tight embrace. Ash's heart raced as she felt his arms around her, his breath warm against her skin. She froze, shock and disbelief rendering her momentarily immobile.

As he held her close, he leaned in, pressing his lips to her face in a series of unwelcome kisses down her neck. Ash recoiled, trying to push him away, but he tightened his grip, as if to assert his dominance, his power. Ash's heart pounded in her chest as the reality of the situation began sinking in. She was being violated by a colleague, someone she had sought out for guidance and support. The powerlessness she felt in that moment was overwhelming. It was only after what felt like an eternity that she managed to break free, pushing him away with all her strength. She stumbled back, her breath coming in shallow gasps, and quickly fled the establishment.

Ash's mind was a whirlwind of emotions—anger, shame, disbelief. How could this happen? She had come seeking wisdom and mentorship, and instead, she had been humiliated and violated. The weight of the encounter pressed down on her, leaving her questioning her place in the ministry, in a denomination that could harbor such behavior. She had always believed in the sacredness of her calling, but now, that sacredness felt tainted by the ugliness of what she had just experienced.

Digging Deeper

Sexual assault within spiritual communities inflicts deep, lasting wounds on women. The physical violation is often accompanied by severe emotional and psychological trauma. The pain of being assaulted by someone within the church—a place meant to be a refuge—intensifies the sense of betrayal and isolation. Women like Rev. Ash are left grappling with a myriad of emotions, including shame, guilt, and profound sadness.

The emotional impact of sexual assault is immense. Victims

often experience anxiety, depression, and post-traumatic stress disorder (PTSD). The assault shatters their sense of safety and trust, making it difficult to engage in meaningful relationships or feel secure in any environment. The trauma can also lead to self-blame and a deep sense of unworthiness, as women struggle to reconcile the assault with their faith and identity.

When the perpetrator of sexual assault is a clergy colleague, the spiritual toll can be devastating in a more complex way. Clergywomen, who have dedicated their lives to serving God and their communities, may find their faith profoundly shaken. The church, which is often named as a sanctuary of love and support, becomes a place of fear and betrayal. The dissonance between their calling and their experience can, and often does lead to a deep spiritual crisis.

The betrayal by a clergy colleague is particularly painful because it undermines the victim's sense of community and belonging. The church is not just a workplace; it is a spiritual grounding center. When that center becomes a site of trauma, the victim's connection to their faith and the congregations that have been a representation of that faith, is severely damaged. This spiritual despair can lead to a crisis of faith, where victims question not only their own beliefs but also the integrity of the religious institution itself.

One of the most harrowing aspects of sexual assault within the church is the silence and complicity that often follows. Victims who report their assault frequently encounter disbelief, minimization, or outright dismissal. The fear of not being believed, coupled with the potential for retaliation or ostracization, can deter many women from speaking out. This silence perpetuates a culture of impunity, where perpetrators are not held accountable, and victims are left to suffer in isolation.

The lack of support from church leadership exacerbates the trauma. When victims are met with skepticism or blame, their pain is magnified. The message they receive is that their suffering is less important than the reputation of the church or the perpetrator's standing. This betrayal by the institution they have served so faithfully deepens their emotional and spiritual despair, making healing even more challenging.

The emotional and psychological impact of sexual assault within spiritual communities is profound and long-lasting. It cannot be overstated that victims often struggle with a range of mental health issues, including anxiety, depression, and PTSD. The trauma of the assault can lead to chronic stress, which affects every aspect of their lives. The constant fear and hyper-vigilance can make it difficult to function in daily activities, let alone continue in their ministerial roles.

The assault also erodes self-confidence and self-worth. Victims may internalize the blame and feel unworthy of love and respect. This self-doubt can hinder their ability to perform their duties effectively and engage with their congregations. The psychological toll of constantly questioning their value and abilities can be debilitating, leading to a decline in both personal and professional well-being.

Finding Meaning

Addressing the impact of sexual assault within the church requires a multifaceted approach. First and foremost, it is crucial to create a supportive environment where victims feel safe to speak out. This involves establishing clear protocols for reporting and addressing sexual assault, ensuring confidentiality, and providing immediate support to victims. Churches must prioritize the well-being of the victims over the reputation of the institution or the perpetrator. This MUST include financial assistance as therapies that specialize in trauma informed care can be pricier and often not covered by insurance.

Support systems are essential for healing. Access to professional counseling, support groups, and spiritual guidance can provide victims with the tools they need to navigate their trauma. It is also important for church leadership to actively listen to and believe victims, offering empathy and understanding. By standing in solidarity with those who have been harmed, the church can begin to rebuild trust and provide a path toward healing.

To truly address the issue of sexual assault, the church must confront and dismantle the patriarchal structures that perpetuate abuse. This involves challenging the power dynamics that allow clergy members to exploit their positions of authority. Churches must implement rigorous training on gender sensitivity and abuse prevention, ensuring that all members understand the importance of consent and respect.

Promoting women to leadership positions is also critical. Although this is not a fix-all, as women are indoctrinated with misogynistic tendencies too, it is true that when women are represented in decision-making roles, it helps to shift the power balance and create a more equitable environment. Encouraging diverse voices in leadership can lead to more inclusive policies and practices, fostering a culture of respect and accountability.

The path to healing from sexual assault is deeply personal and often arduous. For women like Rev. Ash, it requires reclaiming their sense of self-worth and reaffirming their faith. Spiritual practices such as prayer, meditation, and communal worship can be powerful tools in this healing process. Engaging in open and honest dialogue about their experiences can also facilitate emotional and spiritual recovery.

As a community, it is imperative to support women in their healing journeys. This involves not only providing practical resources and emotional support but also fostering an environment where women feel valued and respected. By actively working towards reconciliation and justice, spiritual communities can begin to heal the deep wounds of sexual assault and move towards a more inclusive and equitable future.

The impact of sexual assault on women in spiritual communities is profound and far-reaching. It undermines their emotional well-being, spiritual health, and professional efficacy. Addressing this issue requires a multifaceted approach, involving individual support, community education, and systemic reforms.

Next Steps

We must recognize the deep harm caused by sexual assault and commit to creating spaces where women feel safe, respected, and valued. This journey requires courage, empathy, and unwavering dedication to the principles of justice and equality. By standing together in solidarity and taking decisive action, we can begin to dismantle the structures of abuse and build a more just and compassionate spiritual community for all.

Here's what you might consider doing next:

An important note before engaging in this work...

These exercises are intended to foster critical thinking, empathy, and open dialogue about the impact of sexual assault against women, empowering participants to recognize and challenge such behavior in their own lives and communities. Be tender in this work. Offer check-ins regularly for those that might have big feelings coming up in response to what is offered here.

Reflective Journaling and Group Sharing

- Activity: Begin with a reflective journaling exercise where each participant writes down their thoughts and feelings about the chapter on assault. Encourage them to focus on their personal reactions, any discomfort, and what they feel compelled to do moving forward.
- Group Sharing: After journaling, form small groups and invite participants to share their reflections. This exercise is designed to create a space where individuals can process their emotions in a supportive environment.

- Discussion Prompt: Ask participants to consider how they can contribute to creating safer spaces within their own communities and what steps they might take to support survivors.

Create a Safe Space/Abuse Prevention Pledge and/or Covenant

- Activity: As a group, develop a "Safe Space Pledge" that outlines commitments to creating a safer, more inclusive environment within the church. This could include promises to listen to survivors, confront harmful behaviors, and advocate for systemic change.
- Group Discussion: Discuss what should be included in the pledge. Encourage participants to think about both individual actions and community-wide initiatives.
- Implementation: After the pledge is created, have participants sign it and discuss ways to implement and uphold these commitments in their respective communities.

Mindful Listening Circles

- Activity: Form a listening circle where participants take turns sharing their thoughts on the chapter, especially focusing on the emotional impact and any personal connections to the material. The emphasis is on listening without interrupting, advising, or judging.
- Guided Reflection: After everyone has shared, guide the group in reflecting on what they've heard. Discuss the importance of mindful listening in supporting survivors of assault and creating a culture of empathy and understanding within the church.
- Action Steps: Conclude by identifying concrete actions the group can take to foster a more supportive and attentive community.

Mapping Support Networks

- Activity: Have participants map out the existing support networks within their church or community for survivors of assault. This should include formal resources (counseling services, support groups) and informal support (trusted individuals, safe spaces).
- Gap Analysis: In small groups, discuss the strengths and weaknesses of these networks. Identify any gaps in support and brainstorm ways to fill them.
- Action Plan: Develop an action plan to strengthen the support networks, including advocating for new resources, improving communication about existing services, and fostering a culture that encourages seeking help.

Educational Outreach Planning

- Activity: Task the group with developing an educational outreach program that addresses assault and harassment within the church. This could include workshops, seminars, or informational materials.
- Small Group Work: Divide into teams to focus on different aspects of the program: content development, audience engagement, logistics, and evaluation.
- Presentation and Feedback: Each team presents their plan to the larger group for feedback and refinement. Discuss how to implement these programs effectively within their communities.

These exercises are designed to be practical, engaging, and transformative, helping groups move from discussion to action in a meaningful way. They focus on building empathy, fostering accountability, and creating lasting change within spiritual communities.

References

Davis, L. (1990). *The courage to heal workbook: For women and men survivors of child sexual abuse.* Harper & Row.

FaithTrust Institute. (n.d.). Retrieved from https://www.faithtrustinstitute.org/

Froehlich, K. (2019). *Women in ministry: The quest for gender equality and empowerment.* Abingdon Press.

Gilligan, C., Spencer, R., Weinberg, M. K., & Bertsch, T. (2003). On the listening guide: A voice-centered relational method. In *Emerging methods in psychology* (pp. 253-271).

Herman, J. (2015). *Trauma and recovery: The aftermath of violence—From domestic abuse to political terror.* Basic Books.

National Sexual Violence Resource Center. (n.d.). Retrieved from https://www.nsvrc.org/

RAINN (Rape, Abuse & Incest National Network). (n.d.). Retrieved from https://www.rainn.org/

Suarez, C. (2018). *The power manual: How to master complex power dynamics.* New Society Publishers.

Trible, P., & Russell, L. M. (Eds.). (2003). *Faith and feminism: Ecumenical essays.* Westminster John Knox Press.

WOCN, Inc. (n.d.). Retrieved from https://wocninc.org/

Younger, H. R. (2021). *The art of active listening: How people at work feel heard, valued, and understood.* Page Two Books, Inc.

AFTERWORD: A VISION OF HOPE AND CHANGE

There is no thing as a single-issue struggle because we do not live single-issue lives.

AUDRE LORDE

As you come to the end of this book, please know that you now stand on the threshold of possibility. The pages before this have been filled with the hard truths of the church's complicity in upholding systems of patriarchy, sexism, and abuse—truths that, for too long, have been silenced, ignored, or dismissed. These stories, reflections, and practical exercises have invited you, dear reader, into a deep reckoning with the harm that women, particularly women in ministry, have endured. The weight of these realities are immense, but acknowledging them is a crucial first step toward healing.

What might the church look like when this work is truly embraced? What does a faith community look like that is committed to transformation rather than perpetuation of harm?

Imagine walking into a church where equality is not just spoken of in sermons but lived out in every aspect of the community's life.

AFTERWORD: A VISION OF HOPE AND CHANGE

The leadership is diverse, reflecting the rich multiplicity of gender, race, and experience. Women's voices are not just included—they are central, valued for their wisdom, insight, and authority. In this church, no one is asked to shrink themselves or adopt coping mechanisms just to survive; rather, every person is empowered to step fully into their gifts without fear of being objectified, belittled, or dismissed.

The future church is one where accountability is woven into the very fabric of the institution. Leaders, regardless of gender, actively confront and dismantle the biases they have internalized, holding themselves and each other responsible for their actions and decisions. There is no longer a culture of protection for those who wield power; instead, transparency, honesty, and humility are the bedrocks of leadership. The structures that once perpetuated abuse and discrimination have been reimagined, ensuring that all voices are heard, and that justice is not delayed but pursued with urgency and compassion.

This vision of the church is not utopian, nor is it perfect. Human communities will always have flaws and imperfections. But the aim is not perfection—it is real, tangible change. It is creating a space where harm is acknowledged, where wrongs are made right, and where healing is not just a distant hope but a daily practice. It is a church that knows its work is never finished but is committed to the ongoing journey of becoming more just, more inclusive, and more Christ-like in its love for all.

In this future church, allyship is not a buzzword; it is a lived reality. Men are not defensive or dismissive when women speak of their experiences. Instead, they lean in, listen deeply, and respond with empathy and action. Pay inequality, harassment, and assault are no longer tolerated in any form, and policies have been put in place to ensure equity and safety for all. Marginalized voices are not just welcomed—they are celebrated, shaping the church's direction and vision.

We are working toward a church that understands that liberation is collective. When women, particularly those who have been

AFTERWORD: A VISION OF HOPE AND CHANGE

marginalized, are free to lead and thrive, the entire community is lifted. This church is one where everyone—no matter their gender, race, or background—can bring their full selves into the life of the church and be met with dignity, respect, and love.

This work is not easy, and it will not be completed overnight. But the seeds of change have been planted, and with every small step toward justice, healing, and reconciliation, we move closer to this vision. The path is long, and there will be setbacks, but the destination is worth the journey. Together, we can create a church that reflects the heart of Christ—a church where all are seen, all are valued, and all are free to flourish.

Let this be our hope and our commitment: that the reflections and suggestions offered in these pages are not just words but catalysts for real, lasting change. Let us continue the work, with humility and persistence, believing that the future we long for is possible, and it is already beginning in us.